0704543

My FUTURE CAREER

Working in

Travel and Tourism

Margaret McAlpine

GS

GARETH STEVENS PUBLISHING

A World Almanac
Education Group Company

Please visit our web site at: **www.garethstevens.com**
For a free color catalog describing Gareth Stevens Publishing's
list of high-quality books and multimedia programs, call
1-800-542-2595 (USA) or 1-800-387-3178 (Canada).
Gareth Stevens Publishing's fax: (414) 332-3567.

Library of Congress Cataloging-in-Publication Data

McAlpine, Margaret.
    Working in travel and tourism / Margaret McAlpine.
       p. cm. — (My future career)
    Includes bibliographical references and index.
    ISBN 0-8368-4239-1 (lib. bdg.)
    1. Tourism—Vocational guidance—Juvenile literature. I. Title.
  G155.5.M35   2004
  910'.23—dc22   2004045228

This edition first published in 2005 by
Gareth Stevens Publishing
A World Almanac Education Group Company
330 West Olive Street, Suite 100
Milwaukee, Wisconsin 53212 USA

This U.S. edition copyright © 2005 by Gareth Stevens, Inc. Original
edition copyright © 2004 by Hodder Wayland. First published in 2004
by Hodder Wayland, an imprint of Hodder Children's Books.

Editor: Gus Gedatus
Inside design: Peta Morey and Fiona Webb
Cover design: Melissa Valuch

Picture Credits
Corbis: Bernard Annebicque 13; David Ball 29; Dave Bartruff 8; Richard Bickel 43(b);
Corbis cover, 19(t), 31, 53; Richard E. Cummins 20; Darama 52; Tony Demin 48;
Najiah Feanny-Hicks 17; Jon Feingersh 36; Firefly Productions 12; Patrik Giardino 14;
Sally Wiener Grotta 56; Edward Holub 38; Jose Luis Pelaez, Inc. 45; Michael Keller 49;
Kelly/Mooney 33; Earl Kowall 6; Claudia Kunin 50; Lew Long 15; Daniel Mirer 28;
Frederic Neema 27(b); Richard T. Nowitz 21, 55; Gabe Palmer 46, 47; Barbara
Peacock 24; Steve Prezant 59(b); Carl Purcell 54; Neil Rabinowitz 7, 11(t); Roger
Ressmeyer 41; Connie Ricca 40; Daniel Samuel Robbins 4, 39; Bob Rowan 22, 25,
27(t); Kevin Schafer 11(b); Alan Schein 30; George Shelley 44, 51; Ariel Skelley 35(b),
43(t); Paul A. Souders 9; Tom Stewart 57; Dann Tardif 35(t); Larry Williams 5, 32,
37, 59(t); Eric K. K. Yu 23. **Getty Images:** 16, 19(b).

Printed in China

1 2 3 4 5 6 7 8 9 08 07 06 05 04

Contents

Words that appear in the text in **bold**
type are defined in the glossary.

Cruise Ship Officer

What is a cruise ship officer?

Cruise ship officers work on ships that carry people rather than **cargo**. The passengers on board a cruise ship have the opportunity to enjoy social activities, delicious food, and top-quality entertainment. At the same time, they visit different places of interest around the world and enjoy sightseeing on dry land.

Cruise ships usually sail around a particular area, such as the Caribbean Sea or the Mediterranean Sea, stopping off at different ports during the day and sailing through the night. While passengers enjoy themselves, often until late at night, the staff on board works hard to make sure that everything runs smoothly. The captain is in charge of the entire ship and its crew. Aboard ship, the captain's word is final.

It takes a great deal of work to keep a huge cruise ship running safely and smoothly.

Floating Resorts

With more people than ever taking vacations several times a year, cruises are becoming very popular. Many modern cruise ships are like floating **resorts**. They feature **casinos**, live entertainment, movie theaters, beauty salons, fitness centers, shops, and even golf courses. Each cruise ship has hundreds of staff members to make sure that passengers stay safe, have fun on board ship, and dock on time at each port along the way.

Cruise ship officers supervise the deck and engine operations on board ships. As a ship sails from port to port, it is the responsibility of the deck crew to ensure that the **navigation** is accurate so the ship keeps to its planned route. The engine room crew ensures that the machinery and equipment that power the ship are in good working condition.

As passengers relax, the ship sails to the next port.

Cruise ship officers spend long periods of time at sea, followed by breaks of **leave** or vacation. After four months at sea, for example, a cruise ship officer might have two months off.

Main responsibilities of a cruise ship officer

The cruise ship officers in charge of deck and engine operations have very different jobs to do.

Deck officers, or navigation officers, usually have to:

- steer the ship, using the latest **satellite** and **radar** navigation technology
- check the ship's speed and the amount of fuel it uses
- consult weather reports
- study navigation routes
- keep in touch with the cruise line's headquarters and the different ports by satellite communication
- supervise crew members
- look after any administrative, **commercial**, or legal matters that come up while at sea
- **socialize** with passengers to make sure they are enjoying themselves

Officers often get together with passengers at mealtime.

Good Points and Bad Points

"There's nothing like watching the Sun rise or set from the **bridge** of a ship."

"We are encouraged to socialize with passengers and attend functions. It's part of the job, but, to be honest, it can be quite boring after a while. I find myself answering the same questions over and over again about what life is like on board ship."

The captain of a cruise ship is often assisted by a staff captain, who manages the crew. After the staff captain, authority falls to the first, second, and third officers.

Engineering officers usually work under a chief engineer. Their duties include:

- running and maintaining the ship's engines, pumps, and fuel systems
- ensuring that all equipment is in good working order and making any necessary repairs
- making sure that elevators and cranes, and the **ventilation**, refrigeration, and sewage treatment systems, are regularly **overhauled** and repaired

Because a ship at sea must be maintained around the clock, cruise ship officers work on a shift system, usually working two shifts of four hours on and eight hours off during a twenty-four-hour period.

Once a ship is at sea, all repair and maintenance work is the responsibility of the crew.

Main qualifications of a cruise ship officer

Technical knowledge

Deck and engine room jobs include the use and maintenance of modern electrical and mechanical systems. Officers undergo intensive training to be sure they can deal with any technical problems that arise. Once at sea, officers must rely on their own training to help them deal with difficult situations.

Teamwork

Officers work closely with the members of their crew. A ship's crew is likely to be made up of people from many different countries. It is important to get along well with everyone and enjoy working as part of a team. This skill is vital on board a ship, where people live and work together for long periods of time.

A ship's officers must know the particular skills of all their crew members and be willing to call on them for help.

Communication skills

Cruise ship officers need to have good writing and speaking skills in order to keep records, write reports, and give verbal instructions clearly.

Self-reliance

Cruise ship officers are away from home for months at a time. While at sea, they have only limited contact with friends and family by phone, letters collected at ports, and E-mail. They must be able to cope with occasional feelings of isolation from loved ones.

Training takes place on land and at sea.

Leadership skills

Officers must manage members of the crew effectively. Having previous management training or experience is a big plus in winning the respect of the crew.

Social skills

Officers are required to meet passengers, welcome them aboard, and help them enjoy themselves. Socializing is an important part of a cruise ship officer's job, and he or she is expected to attend parties and dinners, even when an early night in bed with a good book may seem more appealing.

fact file

Most cruise ship officers join as **cadets** and are **sponsored** by a cruise line or training organization. They study at college for qualifications that are recognized around the world, but they also gain experience by working in training placements at sea.

A day in the life of a cruise ship officer

Jim Bolton

Jim is a twenty-seven-year-old deck officer. He works as a navigator on a cruise ship sailing the Caribbean.

12:00 a.m.   I'm up and on **watch**. I work two four-hour watches every day, which means I work four hours, rest eight hours, then work four more hours. As a navigation officer, I'm in charge of making sure that the ship stays on course.

I'm still finding it difficult to believe I'm back at sea. We have long periods of leave, but when they come to an end, we have to be ready to join the ship on very short notice, which is what I've just done.

4:00 a.m.   I get some rest. Working on a ship is unlike any other job because of the watches we work. Luckily, working strange hours doesn't bother me. I have my own **cabin**, with a bathroom, so life on board is really pretty comfortable.

12:00 p.m.   I'm back on navigation duties.

4:00 p.m.   My watch is over, so I can relax again. I try to read for a while, but I doze off for about an hour. Then I take a walk around the deck and enjoy a little conversation with some of the other officers.

7:30 p.m.   It's time to clean up and have dinner with the passengers. They all want to know what life is like on board ship. We organize guided tours so they can see how the ship is run. For safety reasons, passengers are not allowed to wander alone in areas such as the engine room.

Today's ships are operated using the most up-to-date technology.

Waking up in a different location every day can be exciting but a little tiring.

Flight Attendant

What is a flight attendant?

Flight attendants are responsible for the safety and comfort of passengers flying on **commercial** airlines. In addition to serving food and drinks, they must deal with emergencies and other situations that develop in flight, such as passengers becoming ill. They also make sure that passengers behave properly and do not cause difficulties for other customers or for the flight crew.

Each year, millions of people travel by plane. Some planes carry as few as twenty passengers and fly short distances. Others seat up to 450 people and fly halfway around the world. Regardless of size, every plane has at least one flight attendant on its crew.

Every year, flight attendants see to the needs of millions of people traveling by plane.

Flights are scheduled or **chartered**. Scheduled flights carry business people, tourists, and independent travelers, all of them traveling for different reasons. Charter flights carry passengers on **package tours**. These people are all going on vacations to the same place. Both flights and accommodations are included in the price of the vacation packages they have purchased.

The First Passenger Plane Service

The world's first commercial passenger air service started in Florida in 1914, when a twenty-minute flight on an **airboat** traveled from St. Petersburg to Tampa. The airboat was made out of wood, fabric, and wire, and it carried a pilot and one passenger. This flight started a series of daily, round-trip flights between the two cities, but the service was discontinued after three months.

Flight attendants greet passengers and help them find their seats.

Like members of many other professions, flight attendants must attend special training schools. From there, they go on to find jobs with airlines.

At the beginning of their careers, flight attendants usually work on flights that are less than five hours long. After gaining experience and confidence on these shorter flights, the attendants move on to long-distance flights. Some long-distance flights last twelve hours or more.

Main responsibilities of a flight attendant

The work of flight attendants is divided into two areas of responsibility — safety and customer service.

To ensure the safety of passengers, flight attendants:

- check all emergency equipment and clean up the **cabin** before passengers board the plane
- demonstrate the use of emergency equipment, such as oxygen masks, and make sure that passengers know the locations of emergency exits
- check that passengers have their seat belts fastened before taking off and landing
- close overhead storage bins and make sure that aisles are clear before takeoff
- see to it that passengers follow the captain's instructions, such as requests to stay seated with seat belts fastened during bad weather

It is important that airline passengers know what to do in case of an emergency.

Good Points and Bad Points

"There are real perks to this job, such as cheaper flights and stopovers in great locations. Most passengers are polite and helpful."

"Occasionally, people can be nightmares, determined to make a fuss. They are noisy and rude, or they don't like the food, the in-flight movie, or the seat they've been given. Throughout the flight, I have to be polite and try to calm them down."

Flight attendants' responsibilities for customer service include:

- serving beverages, snacks, and meals and collecting food trays after meals
- making sure all of the passengers are comfortable by offering them pillows and blankets
- looking after travelers with disabilities, including passengers who need crutches or wheelchairs
- helping passengers with carry-on items
- giving first aid to anyone who is injured or becomes ill during a flight
- looking after any children who are not accompanied by adults during a flight, and making sure that, upon landing, they are safely delivered to relatives, guardians, or other members of the airline's staff
- selling **duty-free goods**, such as perfume or food products, to passengers on **international flights**

Flight attendants are responsible for any children who may be traveling alone.

After each flight, attendants are required to write reports about any problems they encountered, such as difficult passengers, problems with meals (running out of food, for example, before everyone is served), or emergency landings because of illness, mechanical problems, or bad weather.

Main qualifications of a flight attendant

A positive, helpful attitude

Flight attendants work in small, enclosed spaces jammed with other crew members and usually dozens of passengers. Some flights last for many hours, and attendants need to be patient and tolerant of others. To be sure that passengers are safe and comfortable, flight attendants must work as part of a team, each member of which has specific jobs to do.

Presence of mind

Flight attendants must be able to handle unexpected problems, such as sudden illnesses, arguments, or upset children. They need to remain calm, think quickly, and deal with situations in practical, sensible ways.

Physical fitness

Flying can be exhausting for passengers and even worse for the attendants, who are working as well as traveling. Flight attendants must be fit and strong enough to adjust to disturbed sleep, swollen legs due to high altitudes and cabin pressure, and **jet lag** caused by traveling from one **time zone** to another.

Dealing with passengers' problems, no matter how large or small they may seem, is all part of the job.

First aid training

When people become sick on planes, it is quite likely that medical help will not be available to them for several hours. Flight attendants have first aid skills so they can treat passengers until help arrives. The quality of an attendant's care can make a big contribution to a passenger's later recovery.

Meals, snacks, and drinks help the time in flight pass more quickly.

Customer service skills

Providing customer service is probably what flight attendants do more often than anything else. Flight attendants must make sure that passengers are relaxed and comfortable during a flight. They need to respond quickly to passengers' requests and be sure that meals and drinks are served promptly. Even when the job is difficult and people's behavior becomes challenging, flight attendants have to smile and be polite and cheerful. As anyone who has ever flown knows, having good customer service skills is a central part of the job for a flight attendant.

fact file

Airlines want to hire the right type of person as a flight attendant, not simply someone with particular qualifications. They recruit people from many different backgrounds. Flight attendants must be physically fit and able to swim. Some airlines insist that flight attendants have good eyesight, without the use of eyeglasses or contact lenses, while others accept people wearing contact lenses.

A day in the life of a flight attendant

Peter Mendoza

Peter is a flight attendant with a large international airline.

8:00 a.m.   We check in for a flight from London to Tokyo and meet the flight crew for a preflight briefing, during which we exchange information about weather conditions, numbers of passengers, and possible delays. I am one of several attendants on the flight. Each of us is told about our particular duties during the flight, such as dealing with special meal requests.

8:45 a.m.   We prepare the cabin for the passengers by doing a safety check and making sure all the equipment is in place. We check also that there are no unexplained or suspicious parcels on board.

9:15 a.m.   The passengers start to board the plane. We greet them and give them a demonstration of the plane's safety equipment.

9:30 a.m.   All seat belts are fastened, and the plane takes off.

10:30 a.m. I offer the passengers tea, coffee, and cold drinks.

11:30 a.m. It's lunchtime — for the passengers at least!

1:30 p.m.   By this time in the flight, everyone has finished eating, and we have cleared away the trays.

2:00 p.m.   I carry around duty-free goods on a tray to sell to passengers, and afterwards, I write down what I have sold.

4:30 p.m.   Drinks and snack time again.

7:30 p.m.   Now it's my turn to take a break and a nap.

10:00 p.m. We're nearly at our destination, so we prepare the passengers for landing. Everyone is straining to look out the windows. Even members of the crew can't get over the incredible amount of light the city of Tokyo gives off. When the plane has touched down, we make sure the passengers have all their carry-on luggage with them. We say goodbye to them as they leave the plane.

11:30 p.m. We collect our belongings and go through the airport's **customs** and **immigration** procedures.

12:00 a.m. We take a taxi to our hotel, where we look forward to a night in a real bed!

After landing, flight attendants go through the plane to make sure that no one has left anything behind.

Another flight is over, and we have to get used to a new time zone.

Hotel Manager

What is a hotel manager?

Hotel managers oversee the daily operations of their places of business. This responsibility includes hiring and supervising a qualified staff, ensuring the comfort and safety of guests and other **patrons**, and keeping track of expenses so that the hotel makes a profit.

Large hotels have enough room for thousands of guests at a time.

Hotels provide accommodations for guests. They are also used for:

- business events, such as meetings, **seminars**, and conferences
- exhibitions, which are often run by societies and hobby groups such as stamp collectors, photographers, or artists
- weddings, parties, and celebrations

Hotels vary in size, ranging from small, family-run businesses with as few as a dozen rooms to huge hotels, owned by **multinational corporations**, that often have hundreds of rooms.

Managers of small hotels are often personally responsible for the smooth running of their entire operations. Managers of large hotels usually supervise the work of department heads in areas such as catering, housekeeping, marketing, and finance.

Ice Hotels

Ice hotels are a growing tourist attraction in Alaska, Canada, Sweden, and other places within the Arctic Circle. They are made from blocks of ice. New ones are built every year and are used during the months when outside temperatures are below freezing. Some ice hotels are very big, with restaurants and even movie theaters in them.

Hotels are popular places for wedding receptions.

In a large hotel, a manager generally has less direct contact with guests than a manager working in a small hotel. Managers of large hotels mainly supervise other staff members to make sure they do their jobs properly.

Most hotel managers have no set work schedule. They work long hours that include evenings and many weekends. Because they must be "on call" so much, they usually live in or near the hotel.

Main responsibilities of a hotel manager

Hotel managers work to ensure that their hotels are smoothly run places that guests will enjoy staying at, return to in the future, and recommend to others.

In small hotels, managers do most of the work themselves. Their duties include the following:

- recruiting and training staff members
- supervising employees, giving instructions, and making sure that people are working well together
- ordering and keeping track of supplies, such as cleaning materials, linens, and kitchen equipment
- making sure the building is in good shape and scheduling repairs and redecorating, when needed
- dealing with customers to be sure they are comfortable and to see that all of their complaints are resolved
- controlling finances by budgeting and keeping accurate records of income and expenses

Keeping the staff informed of any changes in hotel policy, schedules, or arrangements is an important part of the hotel manager's job.

Good Points and Bad Points

"Hotel management is in my blood. I started off working as a night **porter** while I was still in school, and I enjoyed hotel life so much I made it my career."

"You have to love the work to do it, because the hours can be very long. When you first begin, you often work seven days in a row."

Managers of large hotels lead teams of people, including:

- food and beverage managers, who are in charge of purchasing food and drink supplies and working with kitchen, dining room, and banquet managers to oversee meal planning, preparation, and service
- housekeeping managers, who are responsible for keeping guest rooms and public areas clean and linens laundered, as well as checking reservations to make sure that rooms are ready for the guests
- business managers, who are responsible for budgeting and keeping records of profits and losses
- sales and marketing managers, who are responsible for bringing in new customers
- personnel managers, who are responsible for recruiting and hiring reliable staff members

Hotel managers hold regular meetings with department managers for planning purposes and to resolve problems.

Guests who enjoy their stay will come back again and will recommend the hotel to others.

Main qualifications of a hotel manager

Organizational abilities
Hotel managers have to organize the work of others.
To do this job well, they must be organized themselves.

Leadership
Managers in all areas of work need to encourage people
to want to do well. People work much more efficiently
if they are happy and feel appreciated.

Communication skills
Hotel managers need to give instructions to
other people and write letters and reports so
they must speak and write in a way that is
clear and easily understood.

Presence of mind
In a busy hotel, there is sure to be the occasional
crisis. When anything goes wrong, such as rooms
being overbooked or a guest becoming ill, the
hotel manager must act quickly and confidently
to solve the problem.

Math skills
Many hotel managers are in charge of the hotel's
financial records, which show how much running
the hotel costs and the amount of money it takes
in. Managers have to make sure that the accounts
are kept up-to-date and in good order.

Adaptability
Managers must be able to take over in a variety
of different jobs, usually at times when employees
are ill or when a sudden increase in workload requires
an extra worker.

In a hotel, problems need to be identified and solved quickly.

Hotel managers must stay in close contact with all areas of work.

Language skills

In hotel management, the ability to speak a foreign language is not required, but it can be very useful. With more and more people traveling abroad, there is a growing demand for hotel managers who can speak at least one foreign language. Hotel managers who speak more than one language also have better chances of finding jobs in foreign countries than managers who speak only one language.

fact file

Hotel managers may start out by getting a degree in hotel management. Qualifications are important, but employers are also looking for outgoing, lively, sociable people who have a real interest in the work. One way of getting to know more about the job and gaining valuable experience is to work part-time as a summer worker in a hotel, restaurant, or club.

A day in the life of a hotel manager

Anna Holden

Anna is the head manager of a large hotel.

9:00 a.m.   I meet with department managers to **update** them on sales figures. The meeting starts with my reports on room reservations, event bookings, and major hotel expenses. Afterwards, the department managers report to me on what is happening in their areas.

10:00 a.m.   I settle down to writing letters and reports, sending E-mails, and making phone calls.

11:30 a.m.   Time for my daily tour of the hotel, when I see for myself exactly what is going on and speak to as many staff members as possible. The only way to run a hotel efficiently is to keep in touch with what is happening in each department.

1:00 p.m.   I have an appointment to meet the marketing manager for lunch. Today, he is also meeting with the director of a large company who is interested in holding conferences in the hotel. I have lunch with both of them and do my best to encourage the company director to use our facilities.

2:30 p.m.   I lead a meeting about possible redecorating in the hotel. It will be a big job that will mean closing parts of the hotel for weeks at a time, so there are a lot of details to figure out.

4:00 p.m.   I go through a pile of guest comment cards. All guests are asked to fill out a card telling us how they liked the accommodations, service, and food at the hotel.

6:30 p.m.   Another meeting! At this one, we discuss ways of bringing more tourists into the area. Local shop managers, restaurant owners, and tourist officials are also here because the more people we bring in, the more all of our businesses will flourish.

Staff members working in a hotel's main restaurant have to be sure that tables look attractive and settings are correctly placed.

Managers of small hotels must oversee the ordering and delivery of supplies.

Theme Park Manager

Theme park managers control the operations of the many amusement parks that exist throughout the world. These parks attract millions of visitors every year. As the name suggests, a theme park is usually created around a particular idea, or theme. The number of themes that parks can use is virtually unlimited. Many parks are devoted to wild animals, while many others feature cartoon characters, fairy tales, or space travel. At water parks, visitors can enjoy swimming in many different pools, shooting down water slides, and taking water rides.

Water parks are a favorite attraction, especially on very hot days.

One reason for the popularity of theme parks is that they offer attractions for the whole family, from toddlers to grandparents. Attractions range from kiddie rides to exciting, and sometimes terrifying, rides and from carnival games to shops and restaurants.

The job of a theme park manager may involve overall control of the park or managing just one area of the operation.

The World According to Disney

In 1955, a theme park called Disneyland opened in Anaheim, California, on 160 acres (65 hectares) of land. In 1971, the Disney "family" of theme parks began to grow with the opening of Walt Disney World in Orlando, Florida. Disney Toyko opened in Japan in 1983, followed by Disneyland Paris, in France, in 1992.

Today, Walt Disney World in Florida includes Epcot, the Magic Kingdom, the Disney-MGM Studios, and Disney's Animal Kingdom. These Disney attractions take in more than half the tourist **revenue** in Florida.

Areas of responsibility for a theme park manager include:

- finance (keeping records of expenses, which are the costs of running the park, as well as income, which is the money made from customers)
- marketing (finding ways to make the park even more successful by attracting new customers and ensuring that **patrons** will return and bring others with them)
- **promotions** (organizing special events, such as carnivals, parades, competitions, and parties, to encourage people to visit the park)

Successful theme parks have been developed in countries all over the world.

A theme park must be a well-organized operation. It employs hundreds, if not thousands, of people and serves even more. Providing fun is a lot of work!

Main responsibilities of a theme park manager

The general manager of a theme park is responsible for all aspects of the park and has to make sure the park is well-run, safe, and popular. The managers of the park's different departments work under the supervision of the general manager. The departments may include:

Technical and maintenance
Theme parks always need new, exciting rides and attractions. The manager in charge of this department takes care of the **installation** of new equipment and the regular maintenance of all attractions to ensure that everything works well. This behind-the-scenes work is extremely important. The attractions manager is also in charge of safety. Theme park rides can appear to be dangerous, but they must be completely safe.

Rides and other attractions are examined regularly to make sure they are safe.

Good Points and Bad Points

"The atmosphere in the park is great. Families are here to enjoy themselves, and the staff members are always lively and enthusiastic."

"Making sure other people have fun is not really the same as having fun yourself. Dressing up as a cuddly animal during a heat wave is not at all comfortable!"

Finance

The manager in charge of finance keeps accounts of the expenses and income of the park and prepares reports to show how much money is made and spent by each department.

Planning and development

The manager in charge of planning and development oversees the design of new rides, shows, restaurants, and hotels. This person also searches for new locations and thinks of ideas for future theme parks.

Marketing

The marketing manager finds ways to encourage people to visit the theme park, often through advertisements in magazines and newspapers. Special promotions might include running competitions with free trips as prizes or park-**sponsored** sports events.

For kids, meeting favorite cartoon characters is often a dream come true.

Personnel

The manager in charge of this department must find the right people to work in the park and make sure they receive appropriate training. This manager needs to employ staff in the following areas:

- technical (working on repairs and maintenance)
- administrative (taking bookings, making phone calls, and writing reports and letters)
- cleaning and catering (keeping the park clean and providing a variety of food for visitors)
- greeting and entertaining (welcoming visitors and helping them have fun, such as by dressing up in costumes as animals or cartoon characters)

Main qualifications of a theme park manager

In general, theme park managers have to:

- get along well with many different types of people
- have good leadership skills, including being able to make fair, but firm, decisions and win the respect of the people working for them
- speak and write clearly and correctly

Managers who work in particular areas of a theme park need a variety of special skills, including:

Technical expertise

Technical managers must understand the technology behind the attractions and know exactly how each ride works. They need to have an eye for detail so that they notice even the smallest changes in how rides and other kinds of equipment are working.

Safety experience

A theme park must be safe for visitors and employees alike. Health and safety managers must establish and enforce safety rules and procedures and know how to administer first aid.

Math skills

Financial managers have to be good with numbers. These managers are usually fully qualified **accountants**.

Having fun at a theme park can really make you work up an appetite.

A theme park at night takes on a special look but also creates special challenges for managers.

Marketing skills

Marketing and promotional managers need to have good imaginations. Their ideas have to make theme parks attractive to the public. They also need to know a lot about the entertainment industry. They must keep up with the newest trends and be sure their parks offer the most up-to-date attractions.

Personnel training

Personnel managers must have a thorough knowledge of employment laws and must be tactful, even when dealing with difficult situations.

fact file

Some theme parks offer management trainee programs through which people who want to become theme park managers can gain experience. Most people, however, gain experience and qualifications for theme park management by working in places such as recreation centers, hotels, and children's theaters.

A day in the life of a theme park manager

Simon Gill

Simon is a technical manager at a water park.

8:30 a.m.   Even at this early hour, the park is full of visitors. Much of our work is behind the scenes, such as ensuring that machinery is operating properly and running safety checks. If there is a serious problem, an attraction may have to be closed, but we do our best to avoid these situations. I brief my team and make sure that everyone knows what they are doing.

9:30 a.m.   I go on an inspection of park attractions. My cell phone is turned on so that I can be contacted immediately when I'm needed.

12:00 p.m.   Everything seems to be going well. I'm back in my office checking reports. We have to keep records of all the work carried out on attractions in all areas of the park. I barely have time for a quick lunch.

1:30 p.m.   Because the park can't be open all year round, my job varies from month to month. Today is very hot, and I envy the visitors who are splashing around in the water. During the winter, however, the park is closed for several months because the weather isn't warm enough for people to swim in the open air.

Closing the park during the winter gives us time to install new attractions. We also check over all of the rides and sometimes redecorate the park. We work hard to make sure the park is thoroughly **overhauled** for the coming season.

2:30 p.m.   I interview people who have applied for a job on the maintenance team. Keeping a water park safe and in good working order takes a large number of people. All the team members must be smart, well-qualified, and not afraid of hard work.

5:00 p.m.   The last interview is over. The personnel manager was also present at the interviews. She and I now discuss which person should get the job.

Theme parks appeal to visitors of all ages. It's the manager's job to make every one of them happy at the park and eager to return.

Daily technical checks are needed to make sure rides are in working order.

Tour Guide

Many tour guides escort individual travelers or groups of travelers on vacation trips. Others conduct sight-seeing tours of cities, historical sites, museums, theme parks, and even manufacturing plants. The tour guides that are described in this section work for travel companies and are hired to accompany travelers on vacations.

In general, tour guides look after travelers and help them deal with any problems they might have while they are on vacation or sightseeing.

Tour guides who work for travel companies have to make sure that the customers who buy vacations from their companies are satisfied. These guides help travelers get acquainted with the vacation areas they have selected and try to make sure they don't pass up chances to see places of interest.

A tour guide's first task is to make sure that everyone has arrived safely.

The Importance of Tourism

Travel and tourism employ more people than any other industry in the world. Worldwide, more than 15.5 million people work in travel-related jobs. In North America, tourism creates more than 1,300 new jobs each day.

A tour guide may be based at one particular **resort** throughout the vacation season or may travel from place to place with a group of tourists. During a customer's trip, a guide must often be available twenty-four hours a day to deal with unexpected illnesses and other emergencies. A guide may have to assist travelers who have lost their luggage or who are having problems due to being in unfamiliar places. Tour guides need to know their customers' vacation areas well so they can advise the visitors on matters ranging from recommending restaurants and nightclubs to finding local beauty spots.

The main part of the journey is almost over, and the resort hotel will soon be in sight.

Most tour guides are expected to get to know the travelers in their care and to spend time with them. They work long hours, often late into the night, and their work is usually seasonal, lasting about six months of the year. A tour guide is rarely employed all year round.

Main responsibilities of a tour guide

Tour guides who are based at a particular resort perform a wide range of tasks, including:

- meeting people when they arrive
- dealing with lost luggage and other travel problems
- taking travelers to their hotels and helping them check in
- looking after travelers who are injured or have become ill
- organizing welcome parties and other social events so group travelers can become acquainted
- handling emergencies ranging from sunburn and jellyfish stings to heart attacks and broken legs
- resolving customers' complaints

On some trips, the fun begins after the Sun goes down.

When travelers complain about their hotel rooms, for example, or the food they are served, their tour guides must first make sure the complaints are **valid**.

Good Points and Bad Points

"I don't have to worry about where I'm sleeping or what I'm eating. All of that is taken care of for me."

"I like the challenge of dealing with the unexpected, but matters can sometimes get out of hand, especially when serious accidents or illnesses occur. It's very hard supporting relatives, dealing with hospital staff and making arrangements for people to travel home."

If they are, the guides must see to it that the customers are **compensated**. Guides may also have to deal with complaints about the travelers in their care. When, for example, customers return to a hotel, late at night, making a lot of noise and waking other guests, the tour guide must tactfully ask the customers to be more considerate of other people staying in the hotel.

Tour guides who accompany groups of travelers from place to place have jobs similar to guides based at resorts, but they also have a number of additional responsibilities, including:

- accompanying tourists on trips
- providing information or commentary about the places they visit
- dealing with all travel arrangements
- taking care of tickets for the entire group

As part of vacation packages, tour guides frequently offer trips and excursions to travelers, which can include horseback or camel riding, boat trips, or visits to cities, historical sites, museums, and nightclubs. On special-interest tours, such as diving expeditions or hiking trips, guides must have specialized knowledge. Trips like these are designed to help people learn more about particular subjects, such as the history or wildlife of a particular area.

To ensure their customers' safety and enjoyment, tour guides need to know a great deal about the places they visit.

At the end of a vacation, a tour guide must always make sure that travelers leave with their luggage, their **passports**, and all their other belongings.

Main qualifications of a tour guide

Enthusiasm

To be able to encourage travelers to have a good time, tour guides have to show that they enjoy their jobs. They must be positive, lively, and friendly, even when they are tired and could use a rest.

Tact

Dealing with people's complaints is not easy. Sometimes, tour guides simply have to explain to customers that they cannot have exactly what they want. Travelers might be disappointed with their accommodations, but if the resort is full, the tour guide may not be able to move them to the accommodations they want. Tour guides must be able to handle any difficult situations tactfully and firmly.

Confidence

Travelers need to feel safe and cared for. When difficulties arise, such as travel delays or lost hotel reservations, customers expect their tour guides to fix the problems as quickly as possible. A tour guide should try to appear capable of coping with any situation, even when he or she is not sure what to do.

Tour guides are expected to help their customers get to know their vacation spots.

Physical fitness and stamina

The work is hard, and the hours are long. Often, tour guides who take customers out to clubs until late at night still have to be up early the next day and be ready to provide information about local attractions or accompany travelers on sight-seeing excursions.

For any tour guide, safety is an important concern.

Self-reliance

Tour guides usually work away from home, looking after the needs of many travelers, which means they have to cope with being separated from their families and close friends. Guides must be content living and working alone. Although they spend a lot of time being friendly to large groups of people, they are rarely able to form lasting friendships with their customers. In this line of work, opportunities to develop close relationships do not often come along.

fact file

Some tour guides have earned educational degrees in travel and tourism, while others learn the business through on-the-job training with experienced guides. Working as a tour guide offers opportunities to travel and see the world and, in some cases, to pursue special interests, such as skiing, sailing, or art, that can lead to other careers.

A day in the life of a tour guide

Mary Rosen

Mary is a tour guide at a lively seaside resort.

4:00 a.m.   My alarm goes off, and I get up and get dressed.

5:00 a.m.   I board a bus taking tourists who have just finished their vacations from the resort to the airport.

5:30 a.m.   One family is late boarding the bus. To get to the airport on schedule, we will have to try to make up the time on the highway.

7:00 a.m.   I wish the group a safe trip home and pick up the new arrivals. One person's luggage is lost. I phone the airport to see about having it **traced**.

8:30 a.m.   The new customers are settling into their hotels or apartments. They are all invited to a welcome disco-barbecue tonight, and I can tell that, so far, everyone is happy.

9:30 a.m.   Guests are complaining about a lack of hot water in their room. I meet with the hotel manager and ask him to look into the problem.

11:00 a.m.   The lost luggage has been found so I drive to the airport to pick it up.

1:30 p.m.   I sleep for a couple of hours so I will be rested for tonight's activities.

4:00 p.m.   I get a phone call from a family about their three-year-old daughter. She has been out in the Sun for six hours and is hot and feverish. I call a local pharmacy and am instructed to keep the child cool and quiet and give her plenty of liquids.

If she is still not feeling well after a few hours, I will have to help her family get her to a doctor.

6:30 p.m. I check the arrangements for the barbecue and set out all of the pamphlets and brochures for my presentation. I phone about the sick child. Her temperature is back to normal and she is asleep.

8:00 p.m. My presentation begins. I describe possible trips, recommend clubs and restaurants, and answer questions from the travelers.

12:15 a.m. The disco-barbecue is in full swing, and everyone is having fun.

One group leaves, but, very soon, another group will arrive.

One thing that is truly satisfying about a tour guide's job is seeing that all the guests are relaxed and enjoying their vacations.

Travel Agent

What is a travel agent?

Travel agents organize vacations and make travel arrangements. Their customers may be traveling for leisure or on business. In the past, many people took vacations only in the summer, booking their travel months in advance. Today, people often take vacations at many different times of the year. Some families go away during the winter holiday season, while others enjoy several weekend trips throughout the year.

Many people travel for leisure, sometimes even several times a year.

To help attract potential leisure travel customers, travel agents often locate their offices in shopping areas so people can easily stop in, on the spur of the moment, to discuss their vacation plans. Some customers want cruises or planned vacations that include both transportation and accommodations. Planned vacations are often called **package tours**.

Travel agents also organize individual vacations for clients who want the freedom to travel wherever they like. Individual vacation plans are attractive to travelers who don't want to be part of a tour's large group.

The Power of the Internet

Travel agents are facing increasing competition from the Internet. Today, many people plan their own vacations on their own computers. They make vacation arrangements, including flights, insurance, accommodations, and tours, without ever having to consult a travel agent. Travel agents, however, will always be in demand because many people still prefer to have one-on-one contact with a professional when they have travel needs.

Business travelers are important clients for travel agents. Large companies, especially, will often select a single agency to handle all of the business travel arrangements for any company employees who have to travel for business reasons.

Travel agents use computers to find out whether certain flights, cruises, and accommodations are available for their customers. Then, they make the reservations by phone or Internet.

Business clients are vital to the success of the travel industry.

Main responsibilities of a travel agent

When agents are asked to provide arrangements for
leisure travel, they talk to clients about:

- what they want from their vacations
- what cities, countries, or regions they want to visit
- how much money they want to spend
- what type of **resort** they prefer, such as quiet and
  relaxing or lively, with a lot of entertainment

After getting a good idea of what a client wants,
the agent helps the client choose:

- accommodations, such as
  large, luxury hotels, small,
  locally run hotels, or small
  apartments with kitchens
- leisure activity options,
  such as walking, sailing,
  swimming, sunbathing,
  or sightseeing

A travel agent
has to find the
right vacation
to suit the
clients' needs.

Good Points and Bad Points

"I like getting to know people and finding out what types of vacations
they are looking for. It pays to put some thought into what you want
from a vacation, because it will be costing you a lot of money."

"When things go wrong, people are very disappointed, so I always
worry when people rush in and say they want to go away in a week's
time and don't care where they go."

Most travel
bookings
are done
by computer.

After a client has decided where to go and what to do,
the travel agent has to:

- make reservations and supply tickets
- advise the client about **vaccinations**, **visas**,
  and **passports**, when they are needed for travel
- offer suggestions about other travel details, such
  as insurance and **traveler's checks**

Competition is fierce among travel agents for business
travel clients, and companies tend to contract with
particular agencies for long periods of time. To meet
the needs of business travelers, agents must:

- make sure the company's employees have
  trouble-free trips
- ensure that the company gets the most
  reasonable rates for transportation and lodging
- arrange travel plans around business schedules
  by booking suitable flights and reserving the most
  convenient accommodations
- arrange conference facilities, when requested
- reserve rental cars or limousine service, when needed

Main qualifications of a travel agent

Communication skills

Travel agents must be good communicators and have the ability to write and speak clearly. Customers need to be able to understand what the travel agent is saying, and the letters, reports, and instructions the agent writes must be easy to follow.

Enthusiasm

An active interest in people and travel is vital for travel agents. To plan the best vacations for clients, agents must encourage people to talk about what they want, and agents must constantly be reading about current affairs at different travel destinations to know how to best advise their clients.

Tact and patience

When something goes wrong, clients can become very disappointed and upset. Travel agents must be able to discuss difficulties with their clients and handle problems calmly and courteously.

Flexibility

To solve problems, a travel agent often has to come up with alternative ideas. If there is no connection between two flights, for example, the agent may have to look into alternate transportation, such as a rental car, bus, or train.

Some travel agents specialize in winter sports vacations.

With the help of maps and brochures from their travel agents, clients are able to plan their vacations down to the last detail.

fact file

Some travel agents have degrees or diplomas in travel or tourism. Often, however, people start working in the travel industry as assistants. Then they learn on the job, regardless of any other qualifications they might have.

Computer skills

Because computers are used so widely in the travel industry, travel agents must understand how to operate them and use them to find information.

Eye for details

If a travel agent overlooks a small detail, it could ruin a client's vacation. Reservations can be very complicated, especially when they involve different **time zones**. Agents should be able to provide information about the language, currency, and customs of various destinations.

Theresa James

Theresa is the owner of a travel agency.

8:30 a.m. I open the office and do a security check, which involves turning off the burglar alarm. After I turn on the computers, I brief my staff about the the day ahead.

9:00 a.m. Business is slow, at first, so we clean up the office, and I make some phone calls and open the mail.

10:30 a.m. A couple wanting to get married abroad comes into the office. I discuss possible destinations with them and give them some brochures. They are planning to marry soon and want to invite about twenty-five guests. Some of the guests want to stay at the wedding location after the ceremony, while others want to move on to different places. The couple asks a lot of questions. Can they marry on a beach? Will the ceremony be in English? How can the wedding dress be transported?

12:00 p.m. One of the computer stations is not working properly. I phone the help line, and an adviser talks me through the problem. The computer works fine, again, but as usual after these problems, it takes me a while to start everything up and get running again.

Travel agents can help couples plan a dream wedding in a romantic location.

1:00 p.m.   I take a short break for lunch.

1:25 p.m.   The wedding couple returns. They have decided to marry in the Caribbean. I give them some information on prices and different types of accommodations. They're not sure now about the number of guests but promise to let me know within a week. We need to come to a decision soon to guarantee that everyone will be able to take part in the event.

4:00 p.m.   The office is quieter now, so I talk to my staff about their activities for the day, catch up on my phone calls, and do some paperwork.

6:00 p.m.   I shut down the computers, turn on the burglar alarm, lock up the office, and head home. Sometimes, I feel like I could use a good vacation myself!

It is rewarding for a travel agent to learn that people have enjoyed their vacations.

Travel Writer

What is a travel writer?

Some travel writers are journalists employed by newspapers or magazines and paid a salary to write travel articles on a regular basis. Other travel writers are **freelance** authors who sell articles to publications. The money they earn helps pay for their travels.

Some travel writers work on guidebooks, which provide a great deal of information about a particular place or attraction. Others write brochures, which are leaflets or booklets full of information about places and usually full of colorful photographs, too. Travel agencies often hire freelance writers to create brochures.

Sometimes, travel writers work on personal projects that may be accounts of travel in their own lives. Often this travel involves foreign countries. The books and articles that come from these personal projects are often filled with amusing descriptions and tales of exciting and intriguing experiences. They are usually written in a narrative style and include the kind of information that will give readers an idea of day-to-day life in the particular place the writer has visited.

Travel guides give tourists a lot of useful information about particular places of interest.

Continental Drift

Bill Bryson's amusing and thoughtful books about life in different countries have made him famous. Bryson left college in the United States to settle in England, where he became a journalist. His travel writing began when he took a car trip around the United States to relive trips he had experienced as a child. He wrote a book called *The Lost Continent* about his journey. Bryson does not claim to be a travel writer. Instead, he calls himself "a tourist who writes books."

A publisher may commission a writer to create a travel book. By commissioning the writer, the publisher formally agrees to buy the travel book when the writer has completed it. In other cases, a writer will have no commission but will try to sell his or her book to a publisher when it is finished.

Travel guides often include maps, and they sometimes even include bus and train schedules.

All travel writers have their own special ways of working. For some people, travel writing is a full-time job. For others, it is just a part-time job that takes them to many interesting places.

Main responsibilities of a travel writer

Travel writing sounds like a dream job. Imagine researching and writing part of the time, then making enough money to travel the world and have adventures the rest of the time. The reality of travel writing, however, is far less glamorous and suits only certain people. Most travel writers live on tight budgets with no idea of what their next jobs will be. Furthermore, long periods of travel can be tiring and uncomfortable.

Journalists who work for travel magazines may do some traveling, but they usually spend most of their time at the magazine's offices. Their work includes:

- investigating new places to visit
- researching material and writing articles
- commissioning articles, which means finding authors to write articles and deciding how much to pay them
- assisting graphic designers in finding photos and illustrations, and putting together page layouts

Travel writers often take the photographs for their books themselves.

Good Points and Bad Points

"I love visiting different countries and telling other people what I have seen."

"The work can be exhausting and frustrating. Flights are cancelled, buses aren't always available, and trains are often delayed. I get especially frustrated when I'm behind on a deadline."

With the help of travel guides, tourists are able to plan their own exciting vacations.

Writers who work on guidebooks have to gather a lot of up-to-date details, but they often live in the areas they are writing about so they have easy access to the latest information. A guidebook includes information on places to stay and to eat, local sites of interest, and bus and train schedules, along with facts about the history and customs of the places described in the book.

Travel writers who create brochures usually use material provided to them and are not often required to travel.

People who write about their own travel experiences often have other jobs. For some of them, writing is an activity that simply gives them a lot of enjoyment. Peter Mayle, for example, had a career in advertising. After he retired from advertising, he moved to France, where he wrote a book about his experiences called *A Year in Provence*. This book became an international best-seller. Mayle has since written a number of other successful books, including some novels set in Provence and several books on other topics.

Main qualifications of a travel writer

Excellent writing skills

A guidebook author needs to write clearly and pack a lot of factual information into the writing. A personal travel writer has to create a vivid picture of what life is like in the places he or she is writing about so that readers feel as if they are right there with the author.

Mental and physical strength

Traveling can be frustrating, lonely, and exhausting. A travel writer must have the mental and physical resources to cope with the difficulties of traveling.

Travel writers sometimes do their work in remote locations.

Speed and adaptability

Writers need to be able to produce their articles quickly and, often, in uncomfortable surroundings.

Internet skills

Travel writers frequently use the Internet to find information about the places being featured in their work. They also use the Internet to E-mail material to their editors. Some writers carry computers with them, while others may use the Internet cafés that are springing up in many places around the world.

Many people read travel articles in newspapers and magazines to help plan their vacations.

Observation skills

Successful travel writing depends on noticing and writing about details. It is the details that fascinate readers and make them feel as if they are visiting the places being described.

Photography skills

Knowing how to use cameras is a useful skill for travel writers so they can provide photographs along with their writing.

fact file

The journalists who write for newspapers or magazines usually have college degrees and some journalistic experience. The qualifications to become a travel writer, however, are not clearly defined. People who write occasional travel articles can come from any background. Because guidebook writers must gather a lot of information about the places they intend to write about, they usually have to stay for a long period of time in those places.

Maria Hardy

Maria lives in Greece, where she teaches English and writes guidebooks for tourists and travelers.

8:30 a.m. I'm not teaching today, so I can do some writing. At the moment, I'm **updating** a travel guide. There's a team of us on the job, and I'm covering a number of Greek islands, including the one that is my home. A guidebook must be updated frequently. A couple of years ago, for example, a new airport opened in Athens, making the information in all of the guidebooks, about air travel to and from Athens, out of date.

9:30 a.m. I'm using the Internet for a lot of early research. I can check bus, train, and ferry routes and find out whether hotels and restaurants have changed owners or closed down. Local tourist information offices are also very helpful resources.

12:30 p.m. The temperature is beginning to soar, and everyone is resting. I relax in a chair and plan a schedule of visits. Once my initial research is finished, I will spend all my free time visiting places and making notes.

4:00 p.m. I start working on letters and E-mails my editor has sent me. Travelers often contact publishers with information. They may, for example, have found a new restaurant or have complaints about a hotel our guide has recommended or want to report that a museum is now closed on Mondays. Although this information is very helpful, I still have to check it for accuracy before using it.

7:45 p.m. I receive a phone call from another writer who can't find timetables for ferry service and needs my help.

8:30 p.m. Time to stop working and meet some friends for a meal at a local **taverna**.

It's time to send the article off to the editor.

Travel writers have to make sure information is correct before they put it in a guide.

Glossary

accountants – people who handle the financial records of businesses

airboat – a type of seaplane that can take off and land on water

bridge – a structure near the front of a ship where navigation of the ship usually takes place

cabin – living quarters on a ship or the the interior of an airplane

cadets – people who are training to become officers

cargo – goods that are being transported by plane, ship, truck, or train

casinos – places where people gamble

chartered – reserved by a group of people traveling together for a particular purpose, often at a cost that is lower than for individuals traveling alone

commercial – relating to business or trade, especially buying and selling

compensated – given money or goods to make up for a loss or an injury

customs – the government duties, or taxes, that must be paid on goods coming into or leaving a country

duty-free goods – products that are not subject to the usual duties, or taxes, when transported from one country to another, usually because they are being sold on an international trip where no one country has the authority to charge duties

freelance – working independently, often for several different people or companies, instead of being employed by any one particular company

immigration – the act of coming into a foreign country, to live permanently, after leaving a home country

installation – the process of putting a new piece of equipment in place and setting it up for use

international flights – air travel between different countries

jet lag – the tired feeling that results after an air flight that moves through different time zones

leave – a period of time away from a job or a duty

multinational corporations – large companies that operate and have offices in more than one country

navigation – the process of keeping a ship, plane, or other vehicle on its intended course

overhauled – inspected and serviced so that all parts work properly

package tours – vacations for which all transportation, accommodations, and activities are prearranged and have a combined cost

passports – documents issued to a country's citizens for the purpose of traveling in foreign countries

patrons – customers at establishments such as a hotels, restaurants, resorts, and theme parks

porter – a person who carries luggage for people, usually at a hotel or an airport

promotions – programs or events that often include benefits such as free items or discounts and are meant to encourage people to buy products or services from particular businesses or organizations

radar – a system of locating objects with radio waves, used especially in navigation to help locate and guide ships and aircraft

resorts – vacation destinations designed specifically for tourists, which typically provide both lodging and restaurants and offer many kinds of leisure activities

revenue – income, or money, received by a person or organization

satellite – an electronic device orbiting Earth to receive and send signals for navigation and communication systems

seminars – meetings that usually feature lectures or other presentations designed to teach or to train

socialize – to interact with people in a social setting, such as at a party

sponsored – given financial assistance or another type of support or endorsement to help achieve a goal, such as getting an education or participating in a sports competition or some other activity

taverna – a Greek inn

time zone – one of twenty-four regions of Earth extending from the North Pole to the South Pole, in which the time of day is always the same. When traveling eastward from one time zone to the next, time moves forward one hour. Traveling westward, time moves back one hour in each time zone.

traced – searched for by moving back along a particular path or through a particular sequence of events

traveler's checks – convenient substitutes for currency, or cash, which are purchased by travelers to be exchanged for cash, as needed, in the amounts paid at purchase

update – change to reflect the most current information

vaccinations – injections of vaccines, which are usually live viruses that help people resist the diseases caused by those viruses

valid – true or legitimate

ventilation – the circulation of fresh air into and stale air out of an enclosed space, such as the inside of a building

visas – official approvals, usually stamped on passports, to enter foreign countries

watch – a work shift, especially on board a ship, during which one or more officials or employees is responsible for making sure that conditions are as they should be and for resolving any problems

Further Information

This book does not cover all of the jobs that involve working in the travel and tourism industry. Many jobs are not mentioned, including airline pilot, hotel concierge, and passenger services agent. This book does, however, give you an idea of what working in travel and tourism is like.

Many travel and tourism jobs involve working away from home and putting in long hours, including evenings and weekends, so there is little time for a social life outside of work. To work in travel and tourism, you have to like people, be prepared to listen to them, respond graciously to their requests, and give them a lot of care and attention, even when they are being difficult or demanding.

The way to decide if working in the travel and tourism industry is right for you is to find out what the work involves. Read as much as you can about travel and tourism careers and talk to people, especially people you know, who work in the travel and tourism industries.

When you are in middle school or high school, a teacher or career counselor might be able to help you arrange some work experience in a certain career. For careers working in travel and tourism, that experience could mean being an office helper at a travel agency, doing housekeeping at a hotel, or finding a summer job at a theme park, so you can watch what goes on and see how people who work in these businesses spend their time.

Books

Career Ideas for Kids Who Like Travel
Diane Lindsey Reeves
(Facts on File, 2001)

Choosing a Career in Hotels, Motels, and Resorts
Nancy N. Rue
(Rosen Publishing, 1996)

Cool Careers for Girls in Travel and Hospitality
Ceel Pasternak
(Impact, 2003)

Flight Attendant
Rosemary Wallner
(Capstone Press, 2000)

Web Sites

Career Browser: Hotel Managers and Assistants
www.collegeboard.com/
apps/careers/0,3477,8-
015,00.html

Careers in the Amusement & Theme Park Industry
www.ccps.virginia.edu/
career_prospects/
briefs/P-S/Summary
Amuse.html

Travel Writers
www.rolfpotts.com/
writers/

Useful Addresses

Cruise Ship Officer

Cruise Lines International Association
80 Broad Street, Suite 1800
New York, NY 10004
Tel: (212) 921-0066
www.cruising.org

Flight Attendant

Association of Flight Attendants
1275 K Street NW, 5th Floor
Washington, DC 20005
Tel: (202) 712-9799
www.afanet.org

Hotel Manager

American Hotel & Lodging Association
1201 New York Avenue NW #600
Washington, DC 20005-3931
Tel: (202) 289-3100
www.ahma.com

Hospitality Sales and Marketing
  Association International
8201 Greensboro Drive, Suite 300
McLean, VA 22102
Tel: (703) 610-9024
www.hsmai.org

Theme Park Manager

International Association of Amusement
  Parks and Attractions
1448 Duke Street
Alexandria, VA 22314
Tel: (703) 836-4800
www.iaapa.org

World Waterpark Association
8826 Santa Fe Drive, Suite 310
Overland Park, KS 66212
Tel: (913) 599-0300
www.waterparks.com

Tour Guide

United States Tour Operators Association
275 Madison Avenue, Suite 2014
New York, NY 10016
Tel: (212) 599-6599
E-mail: information@ustoa.com
www.ustoa.com

Travel Agent

American Society of Travel Agents
1101 King Street, Suite 200
Alexandria, VA 22314
Tel: (703) 739-2782
www.astanet.com

Travel Writer

North American Travel
  Journalists Association
International Headquarters
531 Main Street #902
El Segundo, CA 90245
Tel: (310) 836-8712
E-mail: headquarters@natja.org
www.natja.org

Society of American Travel Writers
1500 Sunday Drive, Suite 102
Raleigh, NC 27607
Tel: (919) 861-5586
www.satw.org

Index